DATACOM BASICS

by Stan Schatt

Telephony

Div. Intertec Publishing Corp.
55 E. Jackson Blvd.
Chicago, IL 60604

TABLE OF CONTENTS

1 FUNDAMENTALS

BINARY INFORMATION

It is likely that humans developed a base 10 numbering system (decimal) because of their ten fingers. Computers can count much more quickly by using a binary numbering system that reflects their view of the world. To computers the world consists of "1s" (-3 volts DC) and "0s" (0 volts DC). We refer to each of these units recognized by the computer as a bit or binary digit.

While the bit is the smallest discrete piece of information that will concern us, it takes several bits to convey the information representing a single alphabetical character.

ASCII

To translate the computer's language into one humans can understand, a standard code was developed representing alphabetical characters, numbers, and other special symbols in their binary equivalent. ASCII (The American Standard Code for Information Interchange) uses eight bits (a byte) to represent each character, number, or symbol. We will see later in this chapter why only seven of the eight bits are really needed in most versions of ASCII. Below are some representative letters, numbers, and symbols and their ASCII (pronounced "AS-key") binary equivalents.

Alphanumeric	ASCII Binary Equivalent
A	01000001
a	01100001
7	00110111
$	00100100

Alphanumeric Characters & their ASCII Equivalents

EBCDIC

While microcomputers store information in ASCII form, many large computers do not. IBM mainframe computers, for example, store information in EBCDIC (Extended Binary-Coded Decimal Interchange Code) form. Here are the EBCDIC (pronounced "EBB-see-dik") binary equivalents for the alphanumeric characters displayed earlier in ASCII. Notice that an EBCDIC-oriented computer would not be any more capable of understanding ASCII information supplied by a microcomputer than an English-man would understand a Martian. In Chapter 5 we will discover how to overcome this problem.

Alphanumeric	EBCDIC Binary Equivalent
A	11000001
a	10000001
7	11110111
$	010111011

Alphanumeric Characters & their EBCDIC Equivalents

TRANSMISSION DIRECTION

Data communication can be one-way, two-way, or simultaneous. One-way transmission is known as *simplex.* An example might be the screens used at airports to show airline arrivals and departures. This data flows in one direction only, from a computer to the various monitors. *Half-duplex* transmission consists of information that flows in both directions, but only in one direction at a time since it uses one pathway. A computer sends information to a printer through a transmission channel and then awaits the printer's response (using the same channel) that it is ready to receive more information. Finally, some data communication channels are *full-duplex* and permit simultaneous transmission in both directions. We will look at this arrangement when we discuss modems and multiplexers in later chapters. Figure 1-1 illustrates these different modes of data transmission.

ASYNCHRONOUS AND SYNCHRONOUS TRANSMISSION

Asynchronous Transmission

We have seen that different coding schemes such as ASCII and EBCDIC can be used for data. We have also seen that data can flow in one direction or both directions. It is also critical to realize that data can be packaged in various containers. Personal computers expect data to be transmitted in asynchronous form. Asynchronous transmission requires computers to synchronize their clocks with a start bit each time a character is transmitted. With synchronous transmission, computers synchronize their clocks with synchronizing bits and then transmit a continuous stream of data. Since the basic unit small computers use for depicting information is the byte, asynchronous transmission consists of a start bit (which announces information follows), the information itself, and a stop bit indicating the end of the information. Figure 1-2 illustrates asynchronous transmission.

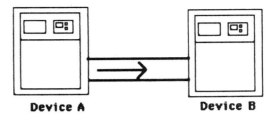

Simplex Transmission

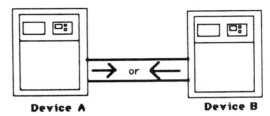

Half-Duplex Transmission

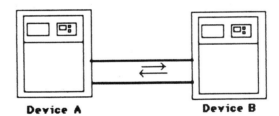

Full-Duplex Transmission

Figure 1-1 Simplex, Half-Duplex, and Full-Duplex Transmission

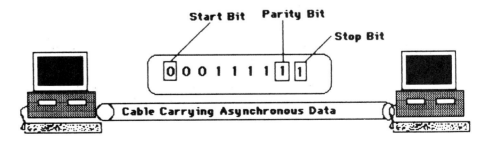

Figure 1-2 Asynchronous Data Transmission

Synchronous Transmission

Synchronous transmission is a method used by larger computers that send greater amounts of information more quickly. A packet of information includes synchronizing bits designed to synchronize the sending and receiving computers' clocks, the data itself (not limited to a single byte at a time), and special control information for error checking and accurate delivery to the appropriate recipient computer. Figure 1-3 illustrates a frame of information designed for synchronous transmission. Notice that synchronous transmission is more efficient since we don't require the "overhead" of start and stop bits with each byte's transmission. Notice also that a frame consists of several different fields designed to hold different types of information such as the addresses of the sending and receiving computers.

Preamble	SD	FC	DA	SA	DATA	FCS	ED

SD	Start Delimiter
FC	Frame Control
DA	Destination Address
SA	Source Address
FCS	Frame Check Sequence
ED	End Delimiter

Figure 1-3 A Frame Carrying Synchronous Data

ERROR DETECTION AND CORRECTION

When information in the form of bits is transmitted from one computer to another or to data communication equipment, there is always the chance that some bits will become garbled or lost during transmission. There are various ways of detecting and correcting these errors.

Odd or Even Parity

Remember when we said that ASCII only requires seven of the eight bits in a byte? The eighth bit can be used as a parity bit. A parity bit is an error check, a way to ensure data was not garbled during transmission. It serves much the same purpose that a small piece of tape placed in a door jamb serves, a private detective. If the tape is disturbed, it reveals a problem (illegal entry) just as a mismatched parity bit reveals a transmission problem. If the receiving and sending parties agree to use an odd parity approach, then the sending computer will count the number of "1" bits in each byte. If the seven-bit ASCII character totals an even number of 1-bits, the computer will add a 1-bit as a parity bit. Conversely, if the ASCII character already totals an odd number of 1-bits, the computer will place a 0-bit in the parity bit position. Figure 1-4 illustrates a byte transmitted using odd parity.

Even Parity

Sending and receiving computers can also agree to use even parity for error checking. The sending computer checks each byte by counting the number of 1-bits and then adds an additional 1-bit to the parity bit position if the first seven bits total an odd number of 1-bits. Figure 1-5 illustrates even parity.

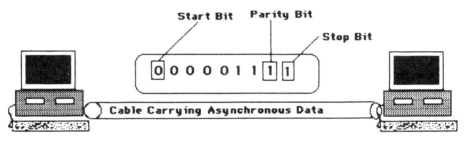

Figure 1-4 Odd Parity

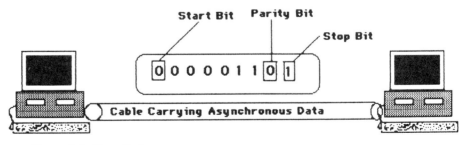

Figure 1-5 Even Parity

The Weakness of Parity Bit Checking

The major problem with using parity bit methods of error detection is that multiple errors might balance out so that several bits are garbled but the total still reflects the even or odd parity bit scheme used. The receiving computer would have no idea that multiple bits have been garbled.

Longitudinal Redundancy Check (LRC)

A longitudinal redundancy check (LRC) adds a block check character (BCC) at the end of a block of data. We will look at two common examples of this approach to checking for errors.

XMODEM

One very simple longitudinal redundancy checking approach commonly used with microcomputer data communications is known as XMODEM, devised by Ward Christensen. The receiver sends a NAK (negative acknowledge character) to indicate readiness to receive information. The transmitter sends 128 bytes of data followed by a checksum, which consists of the total of all the 128 bytes of information. If the checksum does match the total number of the 128 byte data packet, the receiver sends an ACK (acknowledgement) signal back and indicates it is ready for the next data block. Should the checksum not match, the receiver sends an NAK which indicates the block should be sent once again. Figure 1-6 indicates how XMODEM functions.

SOH	SEQ #	128 BYTES DATA	CHECKSUM BCC

SOH	Start of Header (in ASCII)
SEQ #	The Sequence Number for the Block
DATA	A 128 Byte Block of Data
CHECKSUM BCC	A Checksum Block that adds together the contents of the data block

Figure 1-6 XMODEM in Action

Cyclic Redundancy Checking

Many of the larger computers that store information in EBCDIC form use a much more sophisticated method of error checking known as Cyclic Redundancy Checking (CRC). This very complicated method includes a complex algorithm which consists of dividing an integer by a prime number and noting the remainder. The remainder is calculated at the receiving end of a data transmission and compared with the remainder calculated at the transmitting end. If the two numbers do not match, an error has occurred and the message is retransmitted. This task is performed automatically and need not concern us as users.

2 COMPUTERS

A BRIEF COMPUTER HISTORY

The Nineteenth Century English mathematician Charles Babbage began developing his Analytical Engine for the purpose of correcting inaccurate British navigational tables. England may have ruled the seas during this time, but her ships often didn't know precisely where they were. While the machine was never completed, it did have the elements we associate with a modern computer: an input device for entering information, a temporary memory for storing information during processing, a calculator for performing mathematical operations, and an output device for displaying results. While Babbage's computer was powered by steam, John Atanasoff and Clifford Berry developed the first electronic computer at Iowa State University around 1942. We credit John Von Neumann for adding one concept critical to the modern computer: stored memory. With stored memory, programs need be entered into a computer only once rather than having some unfortunate technicians manually set thousands of electronic switches each time a program is to be run. The first computer to incorporate stored memory was EDVAC, completed in 1950.

From Vacuum Tubes to Microchips

The first generation of computers featured vacuum tubes. Its most famous model was UNIVAC, a computer that predicted the results of the 1952 presidential election for CBS based on very early returns. The vacuum tubes were prone to burn out frequently and required cool, dust-free environments. The invention of the transistor resulted in smaller, faster computers such as the IBM 1401. Integrated circuits replaced transistors during the 1960s and resulted in much more powerful, yet even smaller computers. Today, we have progressed through several generations of integrated circuits and can produce a microcomputer with more processing power than the early gigantic computers requiring custom-designed buildings to hold them.

Mainframe Computers

Mainframe computers are designed for processing and storing large volumes of data, often in the gigabyte (billions of bytes) range. They are multi-user and multi-tasking, which means that they are designed to be used by hundreds of people and to run several programs simultaneously. Mainframes often cost several hundred thousand dollars.

Minicomputers

Minicomputers are used as departmental computers. They also are multi-user and multi-tasking, but they offer less processing power, service fewer users, and cost less than $100,000.

Microcomputers

Until recently, it was easy to define a microcomputer as a single-user, single-tasking computer costing less than $10,000. While still designed primarily as an individual's workstation, today's microcomputers feature very powerful microprocessing chips that already exceed the processing power of many minicomputers. New software now permits these computers to be multi-user and multi-tasking. At least for the time being, we'll define microcomputers in terms of their desktop size and their price.

THE ELEMENTS OF A MODERN COMPUTER

Figure 2-1 illustrates the elements of a modern computer. Its input devices may take many different forms, from a traditional keyboard to a pointing device known as a mouse. Computers contain temporary "working" memory known as Random Access Memory (RAM). Information stored in RAM is lost unless it is copied to permanent storage before the computer is turned off. The basic unit for RAM is the kilobyte (2^8 or 1024 bytes). While the first IBM PC could only address a maximum of 640 kilobytes of RAM, the latest models can utilize up to 16 megabytes (million bytes) of RAM.

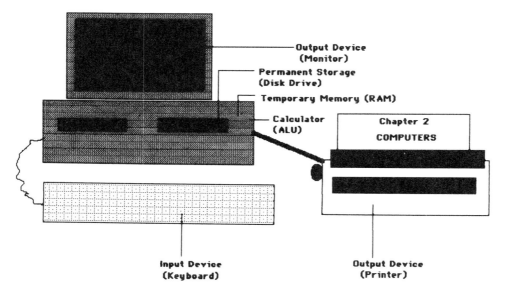

Output Device
(Monitor)

Permanent Storage
(Disk Drive)

Temporary Memory (RAM)

Calculator
(ALU)

Chapter 2

COMPUTERS

Input Device
(Keyboard)

Output Device
(Printer)

Figure 2-1 The Elements of a Modern Computer

Wait States

When information flows very quickly into a computer's RAM, it takes a certain amount of time for the new information to replace the old information. Think of a classroom with just one blackboard. A teacher who talks very quickly and writes just as fast might have to slow down for a time when the board is filled to erase it before adding new material. Computers built with slower (and less expensive) RAM chips often have analogous "wait states" built into their systems so that the RAM chips have a chance to "refresh themselves" or clear themselves before new information is entered. Many newer computers utilize faster RAM chips and feature "zero wait states," which means that the RAM chips are fast enough to refresh themselves and still keep up with the processing speed of their computers.

ROM Chips

Certain key programs can be written directly onto a chip and then placed in the computer so that they are always available to run. The diagnostics program most microcomputers run when first turned on is an example. We call this type of memory Read Only Memory (ROM).

Other Computer Features

Material held temporarily in RAM can be saved long-term through various modes of secondary storage. Examples of secondary storage devices include floppy disks, large "hard" disks, and magnetic tape. We will discuss these items in Chapter 3. An Arithmetic/Logic Unit (ALU) is where calculations are actually performed. The Central Processing Unit contains the "brains" of the computer which, in the case of a microcomputer, can consist of a single silicon chip known as a microprocessor. A computers must also include an output device, which often consists of a monitor or printer, two items we'll discuss in the next chapter.

Microprocessors

The "brains" behind today's computers are the microprocessors that control them. Table 2-1 illustrates the progression among microcomputers from the relatively simple microprocessor that controlled the Apple II (The Mostek 6502) to the sophisticated microprocessors that control the latest generations of IBM and Apple microcomputers.

Manufacturer	Microprocessor	# Bits Processed	Computers Utilizing It
Zilog	Z-80	8	KayPro II & Other Computers using CP/M
Mostek	6502	8	Apple II
Intel	8088/8086	16	IBM PC & clones
Intel	80286	16	IBM PC AT & clones & some IBM PS/2 models
Intel	80386	32	IBM PS/2 family, Compaq 386 & clones
Motorola	68010/20	32	Some Macintosh Models
Motorola	68030	32	Macintosh II & Macintosh SE/30

Table 2-1 Major Microprocessors & the Microcomputers They Control

Microprocessors can be distinguished by how many bits they process at one time and by their clock speed. The Mostek 6502 processed eight bits at one time, while today's Intel 80386 chip can process 32 bits at one time. (By the way, Mostek and Intel refer to the manufacturers of these microchips.) The clock speed of a microprocessor is based on an internal clock that pulses millions of times each second. The measure of this speed is expressed as a frequency in MegaHertz. It is this internal clock that the microprocessor uses to schedule its various tasks. While the original IBM PC used an Intel 8088 chip that had a clock speed of 4.77 MHz, the IBM PS/2 80 utilizes an Intel 80386 chip that can run over 20 MHz. There are 80386 models currently available running at speeds in access of 33 MHz. Before you run out and buy one, consider that this phenomenal speed will do you little good until software is developed to utilize it.

Figure 2-2 illustrates the inside of an early IBM PC or PC-compatible. The RAM and ROM chips are displayed, as well as the microprocessor. The expansion slots are designed to hold circuit cards that connect a computer to various devices such as printers or monitors. We will discuss these external devices or peripherals in Chapter 3.

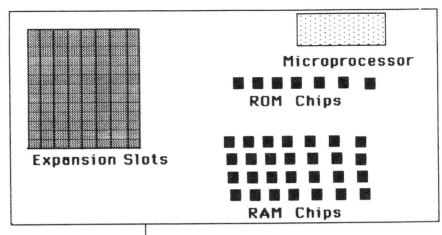

Microprocessor

ROM Chips

Expansion Slots

RAM Chips

Microcomputer Motherboard

Figure 2-2 Inside a Microcomputer

The Data Bus

Closely linked to a microcomputer's microprocessor is its data bus. The data bus (or highway) is the path data takes once it has been processed. One problem with the original IBM PC was that it processed information 16 bits at a time but only had an 8-bit data bus. Imagine, if you will, 16 turnstiles processing passengers to a subway train which only has eight doors. Such an arrangement is not efficient. Today's latest IBM PS/2 and Apple Macintosh computers utilizing the Intel 80386 and Mototola 68030 respectively feature a 32-bit data bus as well as 32-bit microprocessors.

COMPUTER SOFTWARE

While computer hardware consists of the nuts-and-bolts equipment, it is the software, or program, that makes a computer a valuable tool. Computer software generally falls into one of three categories: operating systems, application programs, and programming languages.

The Operating System

The operating system contains several programs which free him or her from the dozens of routine tasks that have to be performed each time a computer is used. Operating systems ensure that a file is stored where it can be located later, that a file will be sent to a printer so that the printer can print it correctly, and that user operating system commands are understood correctly. Figure 2-3 illustrates the various types of programs found in most operating systems. The Supervisor program is responsible

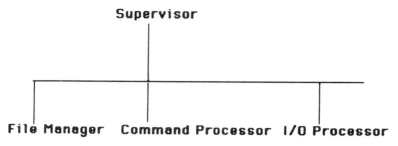

Figure 2-3   The Elements of an Operating System

for coordinating the entire computer system's operations. The File Manager is responsible for making sure that files are named, located, and retrieved. The I/O Manager makes sure that all input and output functions are performed correctly. Finally, the Command Processor interprets an operating system command, checks to see that it is a "legal" request, and then responds by either forwarding it to the Supervisor program for further delegation or informing the user that there is a BAD COMMAND. Figure 2-4 illustrates how a DIRECTORY operating system command issued to an IBM PC provides detailed information on the files residing on a floppy disk. Notice that the operating system provides information on each file's name, its size (in bytes), the time and date it was created (or whatever date the computer happens to hold), and the amount of space left on the disk (in bytes).

```
A>dir

    Volume in drive A has no label
    Directory of  A:\

COMMAND   COM    17664    3-08-83    12:00p
WSOVLY1   OVR    41216    4-12-83
WSMSGS    OVR    29056    4-12-83
WSU       COM    21376    1-01-80     1:17a
PRINT     TST     3968    4-12-83
WSCOLOR   BAS     6656    4-12-83
MAILMRGE  OVR    11520    2-01-83    12:05a
SPELSTAR  OVR    22784    3-31-83
SPELSTAR  DCT    97024    3-31-83
SAMPLE    TXT     3328    1-01-80    12:08a
PREFACE           3200    1-01-80    12:41a
MODE      COM     3139    3-08-83    12:00p
APPLE             1408    1-01-80    12:49a
WS        COM    21376    1-01-80     1:21a
AUTOEXEC  BAT       17   10-26-84     3:47p
         15 File(s)       47104 bytes free

A>
```

Figure 2-4   An Operating System Provides Information on Files

MS-DOS/PC-DOS

The majority of microcomputers used by corporate America run the MS-DOS (Microsoft's generic version) or PC-DOS (IBM's version) disk operating system. Table 2-2 provides a listing of a few of the major operating system commands, which indicate the major functions of an operating system.

MS-DOS/PC-DOS Command	Task Performed
DIR	Display a directory of files
DEL	Delete a file
CLS	Clear the screen
FORMAT	Prepare a disk for use
DISKCOPY	Copy the contents of one disk to another disk
Copy	Copy the contents of a file

Table 2-2 Some Basic MS-DOS/PC-DOS Commands

OS/2

When IBM released its latest family of microcomputers in 1987, it also announced a new operating system known as OS/2. This operating system offers some major advantages over MS-DOS/PC-DOS. It is able to utilize up to 16 megabytes of RAM (versus 640 kilobytes). Even more important, it is a single-user but a multi-tasking operating system. Users may open windows on their screens and observe several different programs simultaneously. Don't throw out your old MS-DOS/PC-DOS operating system software just yet, though. Programs must be written for a specific operating system; it will take a long time for the number of programs running under OS/2 to equal that currently available under MS-DOS/PC-DOS.

Other Operating Systems

While IBM's domination of the microcomputer market has focused attention on its operating system, there are other operating systems worth noting. Some of these are designed for microcomputers, while others are designed for larger computers. The Apple Macintosh uses an operating system known as The Finder. It is an icon (picture) oriented operating system. Note in Figure 2-5 how the computer's control panel, which determines the screen's background color, the speed of the mouse (pointing device), the loudness of the bell, etc. communicates through pictures.

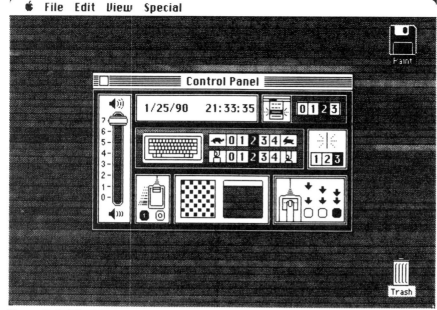

Figure 2-5 The Macintosh Operating System is Picture-Oriented

The major operating system for large, multi-user, multi-tasking computers is Unix. Its features include built-in electronic mail, the ability to communicate with other computers (a built-in communication program), security, and the ability to run the same Unix programs on a variety of different computers ranging from microcomputers to mainframe computers. The price for all these wonderful features is the difficulty of learning this complex operating system.

Application Programs

Application programs are designed to accomplish specific tasks. For example, accounting programs manage the accounting function, while word processing programs permit you to write reports and even books. Many programs use menus, lots of commands enabling the user to select a task to be performed.

Database management programs permit the user to store and sort information in a variety of different ways, while electronic spreadsheet programs enable him or her to ask a series of "what-if" questions. Figure 2-6 reveals a salesperson's electronic spreadsheet. We see that there are different profit margins on different products. The spreadsheet calculates the total commission for the month, adds the base salary, and provides the gross monthly income. By changing the amount of sales for any or even all categories, the salesperson can watch the spreadsheet recalculate the month's total earnings. Figure 2-7 shows the formulas used by the spreadsheet to make these calculations.

Sales Spreadsheet

	1	2	3	4	5	6	7	8	9	10
1			Salesman Stan's Electronic Spreadsheet							
2										
3	Month	Base	Widget	Service	Training	Total				
4		Salary	Sales	Contracts	Contract	(Base +Comm)				
5										
6	January	1000	60000	10000	5000	$2350.00				
7	February	1000	63500	12300	4300	$2465.00				
8	March	1000	72500	15434	7800	$2886.70				
9	April	1000	120450	24567	12324	$4049.05				
10	May	1000	95545	14567	8765	$3122.05				
11	June	1000	102300	23454	17654	$4078.40				
12	July	1000	98654	19435	12345	$3575.54				
13	August	1000	134540	34000	16767	$4883.75				
14	September	1000	98765	19878	22343	$4098.70				
15	October	1000	123345	24340	21123	$4506.60				
16	November	1000	132450	37650	12345	$4824.25				
17	December	1000	176577	76500	5432	$6862.37				
18	Total	12000	1278626	312125	146198	$47702.41				
19										
20										
21										
22										
23										
24										
25										
26										
27										
28										

Figure 2-6 A Salesperson's Electronic Spreadsheet

Sales Spreadsheet

```
Base Gross 'Servic(Train'Total
Salar    Sal(Contra(Contr (Base +Comm )

1000 60000  10000  5000  =RC[-4]+(0.01*RC[-3] )+(0.05*RC[-2] )+(0.05*RC[-1]
1000 63500  12300  4300  =RC[-4]+(0.01*RC[-3] )+(0.05*RC[-2] )+(0.05*RC[-1]
1000 72500  15434  7800  =RC[-4]+(0.01*RC[-3] )+(0.05*RC[-2] )+(0.05*RC[-1]
1000 12045024567  12324 =RC[-4]+(0.01*RC[-3] )+(0.05*RC[-2] )+(0.05*RC[-1]
1000 95545  14567  8765  =RC[-4]+(0.01*RC[-3] )+(0.05*RC[-2] )+(0.05*RC[-1]
1000 10230023454  17654 =RC[-4]+(0.01*RC[-3] )+(0.05*RC[-2] )+(0.05*RC[-1]
1000 98654  19435  12345 =RC[-4]+(0.01*RC[-3] )+(0.05*RC[-2] )+(0.05*RC[-1]
1000 13454034000  16767 =RC[-4]+(0.01*RC[-3] )+(0.05*RC[-2] )+(0.05*RC[-1]
1000 98765  19878  22343 =RC[-4]+(0.01*RC[-3] )+(0.05*RC[-2] )+(0.05*RC[-1]
1000 12334524340  21123 =RC[-4]+(0.01*RC[-3] )+(0.05*RC[-2] )+(0.05*RC[-1]
1000 13245037650  12345 =RC[-4]+(0.01*RC[-3] )+(0.05*RC[-2] )+(0.05*RC[-1]
1000 17657776500  5432  =RC[-4]+(0.01*RC[-3] )+(0.05*RC[-2] )+(0.05*RC[-1]
=SUM =SUM(F=SUM(F=SUM(=SUM(R[-12]C:R[-1]C )
```

Figure 2-7 The Formulas That Make the Spreadsheet Work

COMPUTER PROGRAMMING LANGUAGES

In the early days of computers, programmers wrote in machine language, which meant actually writing the binary code computers could understand. Eventually, higher-level languages were developed, including FORTRAN (primarily for scientific applications) and COBOL (primarily for business applications). BASIC was developed as a teaching language, and is the first language most students learn in the classroom. Pascal has replaced FORTRAN for many scientific applications, while the C programming language is very popular because it is so portable (versions can be transported to different operating systems with very little revision). Today we have very powerful fourth- and fifth-generation languages (4GL as an example) that function as application generators. They feature a number of programming tools that make it easier to customize a database, for example, for a particular industrial application, such as keeping track of a wholesale distributor's complex inventory.

3 COMPUTER PERIPHERALS

WHAT IS A PERIPHERAL?

A peripheral is a device that attaches to a computer. In this chapter, we'll look at secondary storage devices, monitors and video adapter cards, printers, and optical scanners.

Attaching Peripherals

The principle behind linking peripherals to computers is virtually the same whether we're talking about mainframe computers or microcomputers. Generally, a circuit card containing the "brains" that govern sending information between computer and peripheral is placed in a separate cabinet designed to hold such interface cards (mainframe), or these cards are placed in special expansion slots located right on the main circuit board ("motherboard") of the computer (microcomputers). The interface card and the corresponding peripheral are then connected by cabling so that information can flow between them.

SECONDARY STORAGE

In Chapter 2 we learned that computers store information temporarily in RAM, but that secondary storage devices are needed to retain this information after the computer is turned off.

Floppy Disk Drives

Microcomputers generally contain one or two floppy disk drives. Figure 3-1 illustrates the basic features of a 5 1/4" floppy diskette still used with many IBM PC compatibles. Figure 3-2 shows the 3 1/2" hard diskette used by the Macintosh and the new IBM PS/2 family of computers.

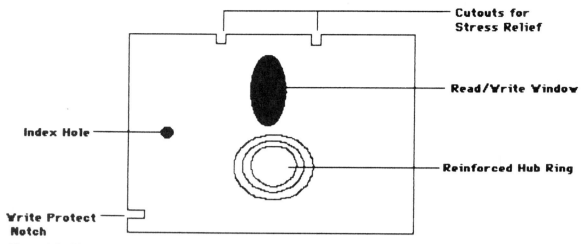

Figure 3-1 The Elements of a 5 1/4″ Diskette

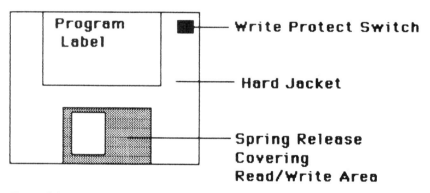

Figure 3-2 A 3 1/2″ Diskette

Formatting the Diskette

Today we buy generic diskettes everywhere, including the local super-market and record store. These diskettes must be formatted or mapped so that the disk drive controller interface card (the brains behind a disk drive) can find specific areas of the diskette to store and retrieve information. Using the 5 1/4″ diskette displayed in Figure 3-3 as an example, we can calculate the total amount of information this storage media can hold assuming it is formatted for PC-DOS/MS-DOS. Each side of the diskette contains 40 tracks. Each of these concentric circles contains nine sectors; each sector can store 512 bytes of information. The total amount of storage possible on this particular diskette after we have formatted it can be calculated:

$$40 \text{ tracks/sides} * 2 \text{ sides/diskette} * 9 \text{ sectors/track} *$$
$$512 \text{ bytes/sector} = 368640 \text{ bytes}$$

We round this number off and refer to an IBM PC diskette that has been formatted to hold 360K (360 kilobytes or 360,000 bytes of information).

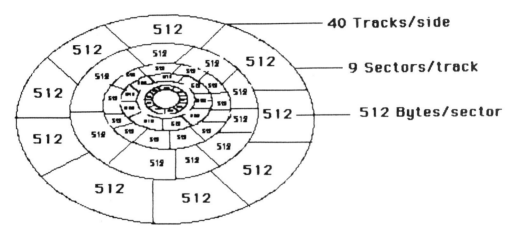

Figure 3-3 A Closeup Look At a 5 1/4″ Diskette

Hard Disks

Often floppy diskettes are not adequate to hold all the programs and files we want to store. So today a 40 megabyte (40 million bytes) hard disk has become a standard, and it is possible to purchase hard disks holding several gigabytes (billions of bytes) of information. A hard disk drive contains read/write heads that travel at very high speeds mere millionths of an inch above a surface of metallic oxide. When we access a particular file, a read/write head moves around a cylinder very much the same way that a record player arm (and needle) move above a record, until it is situated above the desired track. Then the read/write head stops, makes a copy of the magnetic bit pattern below it, and sends this copy to the computer's RAM, where it is processed.

CD ROMS

The latest secondary storage technology involves the use of CD ROMs or laser disks. A CD ROM unit attached to a computer can create permanent data storage by literally burning a bit pattern into a laser disk. These disks can contain more than 500 megabytes of storage; an entire library can be placed on one of these disks. The very newest units are able to create polarized bit patterns that can later be erased and replaced with new information.

MONITORS AND VIDEO ADAPTER CARDS

A computer is not much good to anyone unless it can display the information it is processing. If you look very closely at a computer monitor's screen, you'll notice that it is filled with little squares known as pixels. As Figure 3-4 illustrates, combinations of these lit and unlit pixels form the characters, numbers, and pictures we see displayed. Since the more pixels displayed on a screen the sharper the image, we speak of the number of horizontal and vertical pixels displayed at any given time as a monitor's resolution.

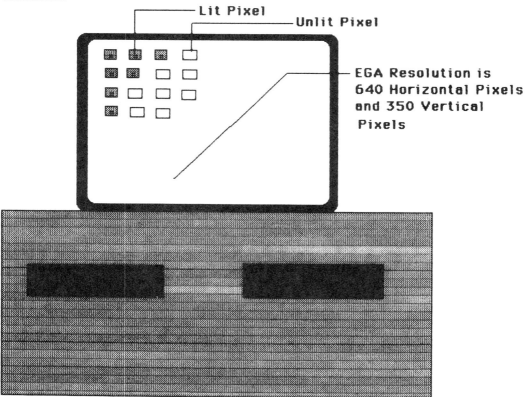

Figure 3-4 A Monitor and its Pixel Resolution

Monochrome X Color Monitors

Monochrome (literally "one color") monitors utilize one color against a black background. Today the most popular monochrome monitors use amber, green, or white. Color monitors used to provide limited resolution, but as you'll see in our graphics standards table, today their resolution is high enough to use for word processing.

Graphics Standards

You must have a video adapter card inside your computer to translate information into a form that a monitor can display. It slides into one of a computer's expansion slots. Several different graphics standards have developed over the past few years, and computer dealers bandy them around as if the whole world understood them. Table 3-1 illustrates the resolution available if you use the appropriate video adapter card and monitor. The other key ingredient is your software. Your software must contain a special "driver" program that sends information to your adapter card in a form it can understand. It will do absolutely no good at all to have an EGA (Enhanced Graphics Adapter) card and monitor if you use a program that only sends CGA (Color Graphics Adapter) signals.

Standard	Resolution (Pixels)	Total Colors	Colors/ Screen
CGA	640 X 200	16	4
EGA	640 X 350	64	16
PGC	640 X 480	4096	256
MCGA			
CGA Mode	640 X 200	4096	256
Text Mode	720 X 400	16	2
VGA			
CGA Mode	640 X 200	4096	256
Text Mode	720 X 400	16	2

Table 3-1 IBM Microcomputer Video Graphics Standards

PRINTERS AND PRINTER INTERFACE CARDS

We'll examine the most common types of printers: thermal, dot matrix, and laser; we'll also look at the differences between a parallel interface card and a serial (asynchronous) interface card.

Parallel Interface Cards

There are probably at least one parallel interface card and one serial interface card housed in your computer's expansion slots. A parallel interface card (still called a "Centronics" card by some old-timers in honor of the American company that first developed the standard) sends information eight bits at a time from the card to the printer. A serial interface card sends a start bit, eight bits of information sequentially, and then a stop bit to the printer. Parallel interface cards are preferred because it is easier to find a parallel interface "driver" program to use in conjunction with the program you want to print. While parallel interfaces are generally not used if distances exceed ten feet, serial interfaces can transmit to printers fifty feet away. When distances exceed fifty feet, special repeaters can be used to rebroadcast a serial transmission.

Thermal Printers

Thermal printers generally use special wax-based ribbons. They literally burn an impression on the paper. These printers are inexpensive, provide almost letter-quality appearance, and are completely quiet. One major disadvantage is that the ribbons tend to be used once only and tend to turn with each line feed. In other words, thermal printers are good for light printing, but can prove expensive otherwise. A second major disadvantage is that they are relatively slow, generally under 200 characters/second.

Dot Matrix Printers

Dot matrix printers use a special printhead. This printhead contains a number of electronic pins that create a matrix; the more pins the printer offers, the denser the matrix and the closer together the dots will print. Today's 24-pin models are capable of producing text very close to the letter quality produced by a typewriter. In "near letter quality" mode, these machines print a line from left to right and then print the same line from right to left. During the second pass the printhead moves slightly to fill in most of the blank spaces separating the dots in the matrix so that the letters look crisp and solid. Figure 3-5 illustrates the difference between "near letter quality" mode and normal or draft mode. A dot matrix model is still the most versatile printer choice since it can print electronic spreadsheets and rough drafts rapidly (often in excess of 400 characters/second) in draft mode as well as print graphs. Still another advantage of a dot matrix printer is that since it is an impact printer (the printhead physically impacts or strikes the paper), it can print multiple copies using carbonless multi-copy forms. This explains why you will see dot matrix printers in retail stores such as The Warehouse printing multiple-copy invoices and receipts.

This is a sample of normal, draft mode. You will notice that it is possible to see the dots composing the individual characters. It is ideal for rough drafts because of its speed.

This is a sample of near-letter quality mode. You will notice that it is difficult to see the dots composing the individual characters. It is ideal for important letters and reports.

Figure 3-5   Near Letter Quality Mode X Draft Mode

Laser Printers

The final printer we'll look at in this chapter is the laser. Based on copy–machine technology, these printers can produce documents very close to letter quality (300 dots/inch) at speeds in excess of 10 pages/minute. Some of the newer models can also print on both sides of a page and in two colors. Today's models house enough memory to print pages filled with both text and graphics. Most lasers now use "down loadable" fonts. This means that a disk containing dozens of different fonts can be loaded onto a hard disk and then accessed by the printer when it needs to switch from Italic to Roman font. Lasers have now dropped down to the $1000 level, which means many small companies can justify their purchase.

OPTICAL SCANNERS

Optical scanners scan a page of text and translate the symbols on that page into a corresponding ASCII code file, which is saved to a diskette or hard disk on the attached computer. A page of graphics can also be scanned and saved to a file where it can then be loaded into a graphics program or desktop publishing program and modified.

A scanner shines a bright light on a line of text and then places each individual character in a matrix. It uses special software to translate the black (where part of the character is reflected) and white (no character) spaces into corresponding voltages. Figure 3-6 illustrates this process. There are two major ways for scanners to read text. One way is for the scanner program to match the voltage pattern in a character to a "library" it has on file of characters for different fonts and type sizes. This method requires a library on file for every font and type size the scanner must read. A second method often used is called pattern recognition. The scanner software analyzes the voltage pattern it has scanned in terms of certain geometric angles and shapes. A capital "L", for example, would match a voltage pattern for a vertical line that intersects a second, horizontal line, forming a 90 degree right angle. Companies which need to automate old manual filing systems with type from dozens of different fonts obviously would want to purchase the best available pattern recognition software for a particular optical scanner.

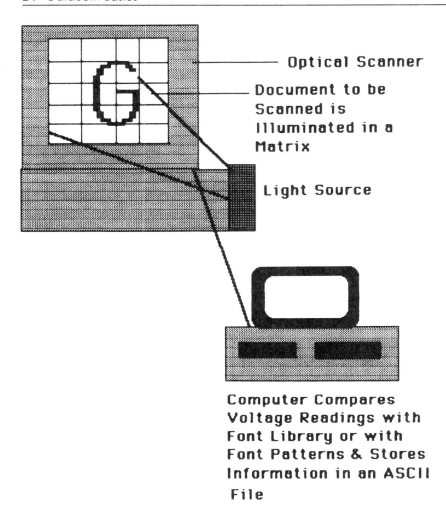

Optical Scanner

Document to be
Scanned is
Illuminated in a
Matrix

Light Source

Computer Compares
Voltage Readings with
Font Library or with
Font Patterns & Stores
Information in an ASCII
File

Figure 3-6 How an Optical Scanner Works

4 LOCAL AREA NETWORKS

WHAT IS A LOCAL AREA NETWORK?

A local area network (LAN) is a group of workstations linked together at one location so that they may share resources including hardware (printers and disk drives, for example) and software (the same program and the same files).

THE BUILDING BLOCKS OF A LOCAL AREA NETWORK

The building blocks of a LAN include a file server, workstations containing network interface cards, network software, and cabling.

File Servers

Figure 4-1 illustrates a typical file server. A file server is a microcomputer (generally one with the fastest microprocessing chip affordable) with a large hard disk. When a network user requests a file or a program, the file server retrieves a copy of this material and transmits it as quickly as possible. What makes a LAN much faster than many minicomputers is that each workstation has a microprocessor capable of processing information without creating additional work for a main computer. It is this concept of *distributed processing* or computing spread out among dozens of small computers that makes LANs so efficient. The file server's hard disk provides storage for all network files and programs. Since files and programs may be shared on a network, a company needs to buy and license only one network version of a program rather than individual copies for each user.

Workstations

LANs distribute processing to individual network workstations. Some workstations may lack disk drives entirely but instead use an "autoboot ROM" chip that enables the workstation to access the network file server automatically when turned on. This approach is more economical (you don't have to buy disk drives) and provides greater security since a user can't copy network files to a disk in a diskless workstation.

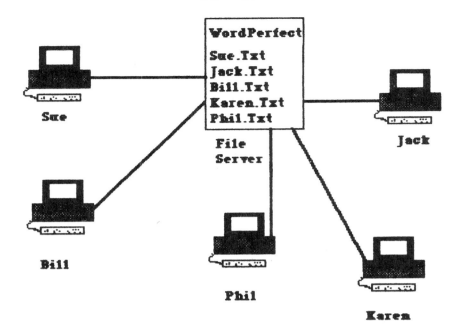

Figure 4-1   Network users share a word processing program and save their individual data files on a file server

Network Interface Cards

Network interface cards are circuit cards that utilize an expansion slot for IBM PC and compatible workstations. These cards contain the "brains" of network operation including the ability to send and receive network information. Apple has integrated the "brains" needed to run its own LAN into its Macintosh computers so that they do not require separate network interface cards.

Network software

LAN operating system software controls network operations the way a traffic police officer controls a busy intersection. As Figure 4-2 illustrates, network software often intercepts DOS requests for use of resources such as disk drives and printers and ensures that these resources are shared. It even sets up queues so that if there are several requests to use a certain printer, the printer will complete one job in the queue before beginning the next job.

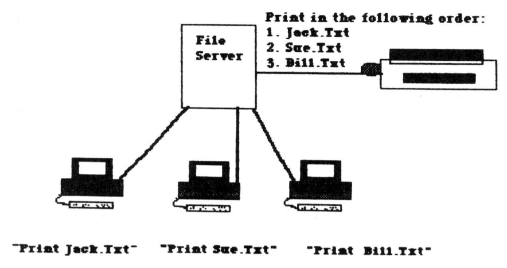

Figure 4-2 Network software often intercepts DOS requests for resources and then provides network management

Cabling

Many smaller networks can use twisted pair wire, which is very inexpensive and often already installed on the premises. Recent advances have made it possible to achieve speeds of 10 megabits/second with this media. Coaxial cabling is also a popular choice since it provides more protection against electrical interference and even greater speed (10-80 megabits/second). Optical fiber cabling is expensive because of the connectors required, but with a new standard known as FDDI, it can provide network transmission speeds up to 200 megabits/second.

NETWORK ARCHITECTURE

Networks can be designed a number of different ways, from the star topology, featuring a central computer, to a bus network in which there is no central computer. Figure 4-3 illustrates these approaches, as well as the ring and mesh designs. Rings use a wire center physically resembling a multiple outlet into which workstations are connected. These wire centers are then linked together by cabling. The advantage of such an approach is that if one workstation fails, special bypass circuitry in the wire center enables the ring to retain its integrity and maintain operation.

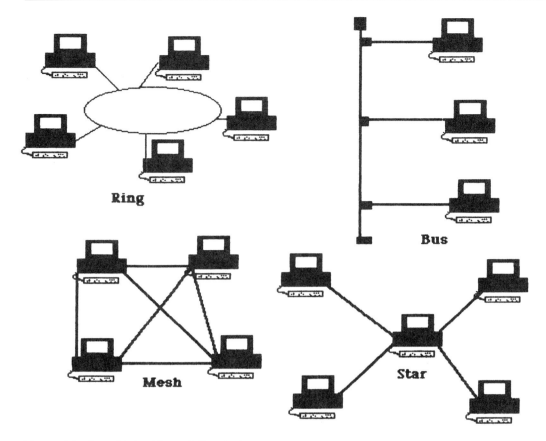

Figure 4-3 Some Major Network Topologies

Contention Networks

Many LANs are designed on a "first-come, first-served" basis much like a bathroom in a boarding house. This means that any workstation needing to send information on the network first checks to see if it is being used; if it is free, the workstation sends its information. We call this approach a "contention" network since two or more workstations contend or compete to use the network. There is some likelihood in such a network of data collision since another workstation may check the network during that brief interval between the time the first workstation has checked and then begun sending its information.

When a data collision occurs on a network, a special "jam" signal is sent across the network alerting all workstations. Workstations wait a different random amount of time (built into their network cards) before attempting to send information again.

Noncontention Networks

Some companies feel they cannot permit any data collisions. One solution is a noncontention network in which all workstations are given access to the network at certain times. A token bus network (the IEEE 802.4 standard) is a bus network in which the network manager sets up a table of workstations using their network addresses. Each workstation address listed in this table receives a certain amount of network time as the network moves down the list. A workstation needing greater access can be listed several times in this table. A token ring network (the IEEE 802.5 standard) utilizes a special bit pattern known as a "token." You might think of this in terms of a taxi that has its flag either up or down. If its flag indicates "Unoccupied," then the first workstation it passes (we're talking in terms of a ring now) can climb aboard and use the network taxi or token. When the workstation is finished, it sets the taxi or token flag to "Unoccupied" and then the next workstation in line can use it if desired.

FIDDI and the Future

Recently a new standard, the Fiber Distributed Data Interface (FIDDI) has been approved. This standard uses the IEEE 802.5 token ring architecture but imposes optic fiber cabling and a technique in which workstations release their control of a token as soon as they have transmitted their information; they do not await the return of the token before giving another workstation access to the network. With this approach more than one token can be circulating at a time, which permits network tranmission rates of 100 megabits/second compared to the IEEE 802.5 transmission rates of 4-16 megabits/second.

Bridges

Very large networks often are not very efficient. If everyone from the sales, accounting, and public relations departments (200 workstations) has to access the same file server, response time is going to be slow no matter how fast the file server's microprocessing chip. A network manager can subdivide one large network into several smaller networks that are bridged together. While all workstations may be able to access all file servers, the accounting department's file server will contain the accounting files it uses most of the time, while the sales department's file server will hold customer data files and sales information. Distributing the files to file servers closer to where they are needed can improve response time tremendously. As Figure 4-4 illustrates, one workstation in each network will contain two network interface cards, one for its own network and one for the network to which it will serve as a bridge. This workstation runs special bridge software and routes information back and forth between the two networks.

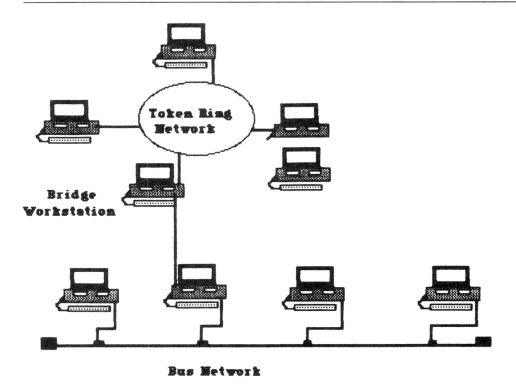

Figure 4-4 A Bridge Connecting Two Networks

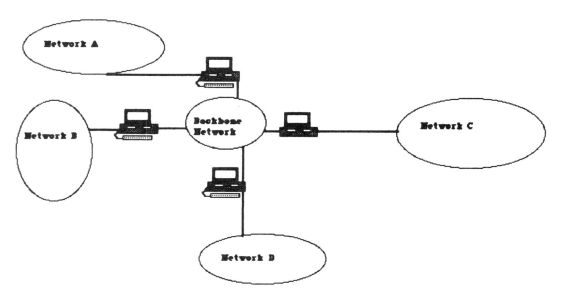

Figure 4-5 A Backbone Network

Backbones

Sometimes a network manager may face the nightmare of bridging dozens of networks together. As Figure 4-5 illustrates, one solution is to have a network composed of nothing but highspeed bridge workstations. Someone (who may have had a bit too much to drink) noticed that this ring of bridge workstations resembled a human backbone, and the name stuck. The backbone serves as a gigantic switching station, with responsibility for routing communications between bridged networks. It keeps special routing tables and determines the fastest path for a message to take. If a bridge is temporarily out of service, the backbone network will re-route the message using another path.

STANDARDS FOR CONNECTING EVERYTHING TOGETHER

5

It's rare today for a company not to have at least a few different types of computers. Add some branch offices, and the chances become even better that the various branches will have trouble getting their computers to understand each other. The International Standards Organization (ISO) developed a model set of standards to make it easier for hetergeneous computers to communicate. For a company purchasing equipment, the OSI (Open System Interconnect) model gives some assurance that computer products from different vendors will work together. The OSI model also prohibits computer companies from "locking in" their customers to a product line. But computer manufacturers have been forced by the public to support these OSI standards.

THE OSI MODEL

The OSI model, illustrated in Figure 5-1, consists of a series of layers, each with its own functions and its own set of rules or protocols. Since each of the model's seven layers deals with a specific set of responsibilities, the ISO can update the standards for one layer without having to completely overhaul the entire model.

The easiest way to try to understand this complex model is to observe it in operation. Let's follow the route of some data that a program running on computer A wants to send to a program running on Computer B. Each OSI model layer will want to add its own instructions (directed to its counterpart layer on the other computer) to the data packet. Each layer will also add some instructions for the layer below it, since under the OSI model, a layer services the layer directly above it. Soon the data and all the corresponding instructions will resemble a snowball growing in size (in this case accumulating bits) as it moves down the OSI layers of computer A. As the snowball begins moving up the corresponding layers of computer B, each layer will remove the instructions directed to it so that ultimately only the data itself remains for the corresponding program on Computer B. If Computer B needs to reply to Computer A, the whole process repeats itself in reverse.

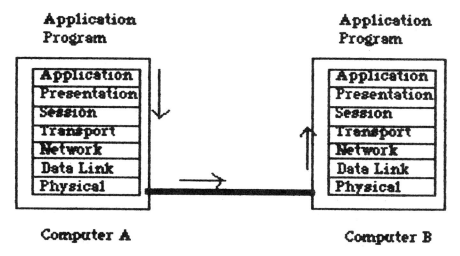

Figure 5-1 The OSI Model

The Application Layer

A program running on Computer A sends some data destined for a program running on Computer B along with some instructions to its own Application layer. The Application layer takes the data and adds some instructions to its corresponding Application layer ("Let's agree to follow the rules associated with coding the data to correspond to the way a certain terminal does it"). The Application layer also adds some information meant only for the layer below it, the Presentation layer ("Send this data encrypted so that spies can't read it!").

Presentation Layer

In Figure 5-2, the Presentation layer has received a data packet containing data, information designated for the Application layer on Computer B, and some specific instructions it needs concerning one of its functions (encryption). The Presentation layer performs its job by adding instructions meant for its corresponding Presentation layer on Computer B ("Let's agree to use encryption method C"). This layer also adds some specific instructions to the Session layer below it, which has prime responsibility for overseeing the type of data dialog that will take place ("Tell the Transport layer not to send the information faster than I can handle it!").

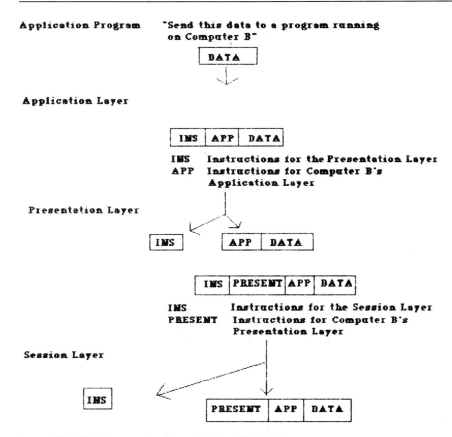

Figure 5-2 The Presentation Layer in the OSI Model

Session Layer

The Session layer in Figure 5-3 reads its instructions and then adds a message to the data packet designed for its corresponding Session layer on Computer B ("Let's organize the dialog between the two Presentation layers so that their conversation follows this format. . ."). The Session layer also adds a note for its Transport layer ("We need a high grade of service and don't let the data flow too quickly. . .").

Transport Layer

The Transport layer takes responsibility for the overall transport of information and the quality of service involved. In Figure 5-4 we see the Transport layer adding instructions for its corresponding layer on computer B ("We need grade of service 2") and a note to its own Network layer, which is responsible for the actual details of routing data packets ("Be sure that if this data is sent by different methods, it's reassembled in the correct order at its destination").

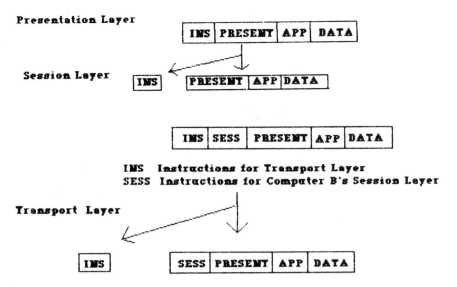

Figure 5-3   The Role of the Session Layer

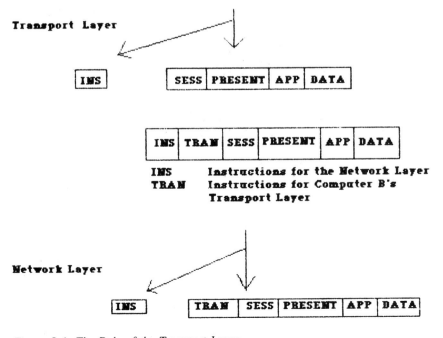

Figure 5-4   The Role of the Transport Layer

Network Layer

The Network layer concerns itself with the day-to-day nitty-gritty activities of routing data from one location to another. In Figure 5-5 it has added its specific instructions to the Network layer on Computer B ("Here's my address and the data should follow this specific route to your address") and then adds some directions to the Data Link Layer below it (Please see that the data is reassembled in the following order. . .").

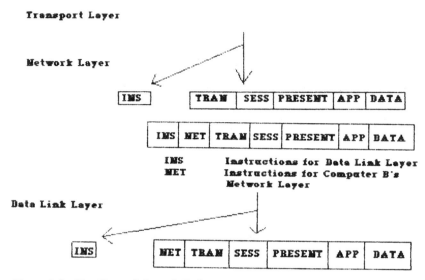

Figure 5-5 The Network Layer's Role

Data Link Layer

The Data Link layer is responsible for error detection and correction, for keeping track of statistics as well as data flow, and for the correct segmenting of bits it receives from the Physical layer. In Figure 5-6 it has added its instructions for the Data Link layer on Computer B ("Take the bits that arrive and reassemble them back into data packets according to this format. . .") as well as its instructions to the Physical layer ("Establish an actual physical electrical connection with Computer B. . .").

Physical Layer

The Physical layer must concern itself with very basic electronics. It has its orders to make a connection with Computer B and then begin transmitting the data and control information it has received as a bit stream, a set of digital pulses. Figure 5-7 shows what happens as the data packet begins its movement through the corresponding OSI layers of Computer B.

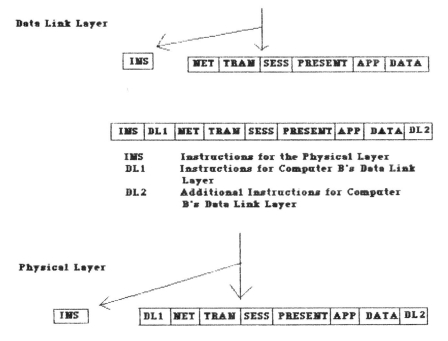

Figure 5-6 The Data Link Layer's Role

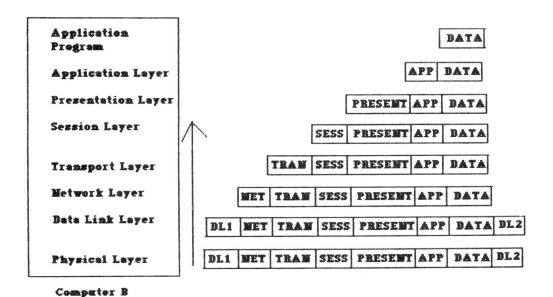

Figure 5-7 The Data Packet's Movement Through Computer B's OSI Layers

Why the OSI Model Is So Important

The OSI model is becoming more and more important because it ensures that different vendors' computers will be able to communicate with each other. The U.S. government has developed a set of protocols known as GOSIP (Government OSI Profile), which will ensure that all the products it purchases in the future will be compatible.

ELECTRONIC MAIL

Most local area networks use some kind of electronic mail program so that workstations can forward memos and reports within a company. Unfortunately, many local area network electronic mail programs are incompatible with each other and incompatible with the electronic mail programs used by mainframe computers such as IBM's PROFS program. One of the benefits of the OSI model is the development of a set of standards, the X.400 family of protocols, which when followed provides compatibility among various electronic mail programs. These protocols are found in the Application layer of the OSI model. One component of this X.400 set of standards, Message Handling System (MHS), ensures that information leaves a computer packaged in a format that another X.400-compatible system can understand and use.

A second set of OSI standards, the X.500 family of protocols, is being developed by the ISO to provide a worldwide common electronic mail directory service. If all electronic mail programs and networks use the same basic addressing scheme, it will be possible for a network user in Phoenix with a Macintosh computer to send an electronic mail message to her boss in Paris who uses an IBM mainframe computer without either user having to be concerned about how the message will be transmitted or received. The entire process will be invisible to electronic mail users who simply will indicate that they are sending a message to Bill Smith at the Paris office of Widget Technology. The electronic mail program will search its worldwide directory and determine the address of Bill's network and his specific workstation address.

Isn't science wonderful? Who said we couldn't develop a more efficient way to send and receive junk mail?

LINKING TOGETHER
6 # THE MICROCOMPUTER
AND MAINFRAME
WORLDS

In this chapter we'll look at some of the ways the mainframe computer and microcomputer worlds can be linked together. We'll see how these "gateways" make it possible for a data processing manager to link together all computing resources and distribute information where it's needed.

THE MAINFRAME ENVIRONMENT

As we saw in Chapter 2, mainframe computers are defined by their speed (generally able to process more than 10 million instructions/second) and their expense. Unlike microcomputers, these units are housed in rooms that provide environmental protection. In this chapter we'll survey a few of the major devices in this mainframe world but defer discussion of multiplexers and modems to the next chapter.

Unlike the distributed processing system of local area networks using microcomputers discussed in Chapter 4, the mainframe computer provides the bulk of the data processing, while auxiliary computers "offload" work that might distract it.

The Mainframe Computer

The mainframe computer is sometimes referred to as a "number cruncher." Often able to swallow and process 64-bit "words," the machine is built for a multi-user, multi-tasking environment. It is not unusual to have several hundred terminals all linked to this behemoth by literally miles of coaxial cable running under the floor. While several companies produce these machines, we'll focus on IBM's equipment since it is the current leader in market share.

Front End Processors

Have you ever tried to get past an executive's secretary? Her job is to screen all calls and help to regulate the paper flowing across the boss's desk. This is precisely the role of a front end processor (FEP) such as the IBM 3705 communications controller. In effect, this unit is an actual computer designed to handle the information flow and routine processing so that the mainframe or "host" computer can do what it does best. Figure 6-1 illustrates an FEP in action.

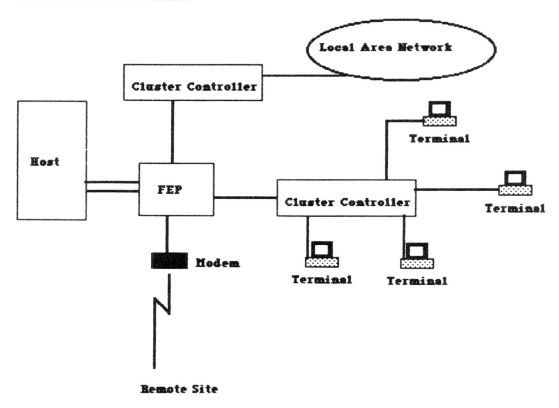

Figure 6-1 An FEP in Action

Cluster Controllers

Dozens of terminals communicate with the mainframe computer either on-site or remotely through modems. The information coming in can be handled by a cluster controller, which forwards it to the front end processor for delivery to the mainframe computer. Figure 6-2 illustrates the role of the cluster controller.

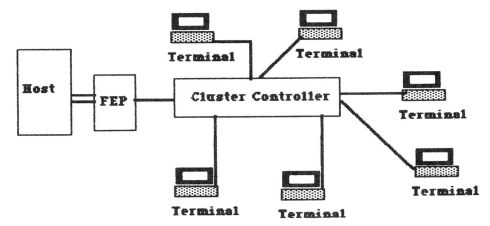

Figure 6-2   The Role of a Cluster Controller

Protocol is Important for "Tourists" Visiting this Mainframe World

Many tourists have returned from Paris with distressing tales of how difficult it is to communicate with French citizens who seem to understand English but choose to ignore it and only respond to French. In much the same way, the IBM mainframe world uses a synchronous transmission protocol called Synchronous Data Link Control (SDLC). Microcomputers attempting to converse in asynchronous mode are ignored. The way to resolve these communication differences is through a gateway, our next topic of discussion.

LINKING THE MICROCOMPUTER AND MAINFRAME WORLDS

Terminal Emulation

At the lowest level of connectivity is terminal emulation. It is possible to add a special circuit card to an IBM PC or compatible that performs the protocol conversion (remember our discussion of synchronous and asynchronous transmission?) and data format (remember our discussion of ASCII versus EBCDIC format?). Special terminal emulation software runs on the PC and "paints" the unit's screen to resemble the screen of an IBM 327X terminal.

Terminals have a number of special keys not found on a PC keyboard, so the terminal emulation software must convert various combinations of keystrokes (a [CTRL] and [F-6], for example) into a command normally issued by a single 3278 terminal function key. Similarly, the software must take information the IBM mainframe assumes is going to be displayed on a conventional 3278 terminal screen and place the information in appropriate areas of the PC's screen.

With all this hardware and software as well as the coaxial cabling necessary to link PC and mainframe via front end processor, the PC is still just a very expensive "dumb" terminal. It can receive and display information from the mainframe, but it cannot process the information any more than a real terminal (without microcoprocessor) can.

A second method of terminal emulation involves a remote workstation connected via modem with a communications controller. Figure 6-3 illustrates a mainframe linked to both a local and a remote PC workstation.

Micro-Mainframe Gateways

It is possible to use a single workstation on a local area network as a mainframe gateway. This workstation is connected via hardware (a gateway circuit card) and software (terminal emulation software) with a mainframe via a front end processor. The advantage of such an arrangement is that several workstations can have "sessions" with the mainframe by sharing the single gateway; this method is far more cost-effective than connecting individual PCs to the mainframe.

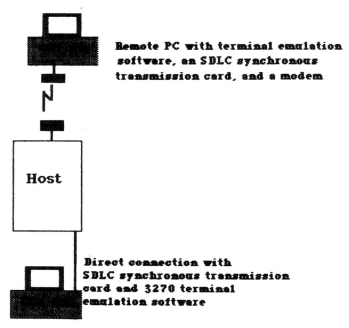

Remote PC with terminal emulation software, an SDLC synchronous transmission card, and a modem

Host

Direct connection with SDLC synchronous transmission card and 3270 terminal emulation software

Figure 6-3 A Mainframe Linked to a Local PC and a Remote PC

Micro-Mainframe Data Exchange

One major problem many people have is transferring information from a mainframe to their microcomputer. Even if the data can be converted into the appropriate form and format, it usually can only be downloaded to the microcomputer's disk for storage as an ASCII file. What the microcomputer user usually really wants is far more than this; he or she would like to see the data flow from the mainframe computer program directly into a different program, such as dBASE IV, running on the microcomputer.

One problem with this scenario is that every program stores its information in its own format. Not only is file structure far from universal, but even the size of fields within a file (how many characters are reserved for the city field, for example) differ widely. Some software companies are trying to resolve this delimma by offering both mainframe and microcomputer versions of their programs. A database program such as FOCUS running on a mainframe computer has little trouble transferring data directly into the files created by its microcomputer version, PC-FOCUS, since the same company wrote both programs. While this solution is not always possible at present, the future may be brighter because of a movement toward something called "peer communications."

Peer Communications

A computer's network architecture represents its organizational structure and determines the relationships of all its hardware and software components. IBM's network architecture, System Network Architecture (or SNA), was designed to handle the traditional hierarchical computer network organization of the 1970s; this meant that devices communicate with each other only by going through the mainframe computer in what has been called a Master X Slave arrangement. In the late 1980s, IBM has begun to modify SNA to include the ability for peer communications, a structure in which two devices could communicate directly with each other without mainframe intervention. The addition of PU 2.1 and LU 6.2 meant that by redefining the relationships of physical units (PUs) and logical units (LUs), the two devices were now permitted to communicate directly with each other. This still left one major issue unresolved, though. How could conventional software address these new relationships?

Recently IBM has released a set of programming tools known as AP-PIC (Applied Program-to-Program-Interface-Communications). These commands gave programmers the ability to write interfaces enabling one program to communicate directly with another. In the future, a program running on a PC will be able to communicate with a mainframe computer and exchange information transparent to the end-users. Two PCs linked to a mainframe will be able to exchange information between programs running on both microcomputers and then save data directly on the mainframe's secondary storage device. An Apple Macintosh version of these programming tools ensures that sometime in the future Macintosh users will also become part of the peer communications movement.

MULTIPLEXERS, T-1 CARRIERS AND PACKET SWITCHED NETWORKS

7

In this chapter, we'll take a look at some ways in which data is transmitted from one location to another. We'll see how, as voice signals are increasingly digitized and sent along the same transmission lines that carry computer data, it becomes more and more difficult to distinguish between the two.

MULTIPLEXING AND MULTIPLEXERS

What is Multiplexing?

Multiplexing is a technique that permits several different signals to be transmitted over a single link. For years telephone companies have sent strands of thousands of different conversations over the same lines. These conversations are reassembled at the receiving stations and then send to their final destination. Multiplexing is also a very effective technique for transmitting data efficiently.

In Figure 7-1 we see four terminals sending information at 300 bits/second to a multiplexer. (Another very common term for this device is a "mux.") The company wants to utilize its expensive line as efficiently as possible so it uses a multiplexer to send signals from all four terminals at 1200 bits/second.

We call this type of multiplexer a time division multiplexer (TDM), since it allocates time slots to each signal source. Notice that all four terminals are guaranteed a time slot under this approach. A multiplexer at the receiving end demultiplexes the signals into their four different components and then forwards them for delivery.

One weakness with this approach is that sometimes the "train" leaves without any data from a terminal that simply does not have anything to send at that particular moment. While the data "trains" always run on time with time division multiplexing, frequently many of the cars are empty of any data passengers. Surely there must be a statistical way of handling the probability of a particular terminal not having anything to send at a particular moment.

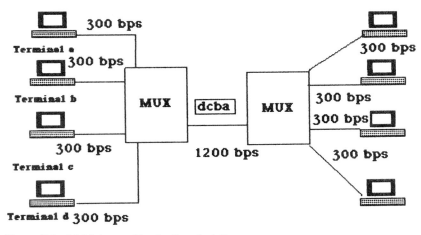

Figure 7-1 Multiplexers Handle Terminal Data

Statistical Time Divsion Multiplexing

A statistical time division multiplexer (STDM) will keep all its data passenger seats occupied by servicing a greater number of terminals, since it knows statistically that not all terminals will have something to send at the same time. In addition, an STDM will contain memory to permit terminals to queue up information to be sent. If terminal #1 has nothing to send and terminal #2 has a great deal of data to send, then the STDM will let terminal #2 data occupy both its own slot as well as terminal #1's time slot. A terminal identifier accompanies the data so that the multiplexer at the other end knows which signals belong to a particular data stream. Figure 7-2 illustrates an STDM in operation.

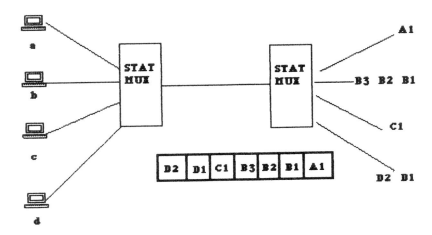

Figure 7-2 A STAT MUX in Operation

T-1 CARRIERS and T-1 MULTIPLEXERS

A Bit of T-1 History

For several years telephone companies digitized voice signals using a technique known as pulse code modulation (PCM) and then sent this information over special high-speed lines (T-1 carriers) from one central office to another. Since PCM sampled 8000 eight-bit voice signals/second, it is easy enough to calculate that a voice channel was transmitting at 64000 bits/second:

$$8000 \text{ samples/second} \times 8 \text{ bits/sample} = 64000 \text{ bits/second:}$$

Since the telephone company's special T-1 lines were capable of carrying 24 of these voice conversations at one time along with eight bits of special control information (error checking, etc.), they could carry a total of 1.5444 million bits/second:

$$64000 \text{ bits/second/channel} \times 24 \text{ channels} = 1.536 \text{ mbs}$$

$$8 \text{ bits/second/sample} \times 8000 \text{ samples/second} = \underline{64000 \text{ bps}}$$

$$\text{Total} \qquad\qquad 1.544 \text{ mbs}$$

While we will continue to refer to a T-1 line, Figure 7-3 reveals that there are other possible line sizes. Today it is quite common for companies to lease T-1 lines from their local phone company expressly for the transmission of their own high-speed data. Special T-1 multiplexers can multiplex several different data signals over these 24 channels.

Signal	Speed (Mbps)	Number of T1 Channels
DS-0	.064	.042
DS-1	1.544	1
DS-2	6.312	4
DS-3	45	28
DS-4	274	168

Figure 7-3 T-1 Options

A very recent development is the availability of fractional T-1 lines. Smaller companies can now lease a small fraction of the 24 channels comprising a T-1 line. Data-processing managers who now use several dedicated phone lines to transmit data at, say, 19,200 bits/second may find it much more cost-effective to use fractional T-1 service.

One problem with T-1 service is that T-1 lines are not found in all areas. It is prohibitively expensive to have to pay the costs of a new T-1 line installation.

PACKET SWITCHED NETWORKS

A company that needs to transmit data between two sales offices has at least three different options. One choice is to use modems at both locations to send data over the public telephone system; unfortunately, such information travels relatively slowly at a maximum of 19,200 bps in asynchronous mode and 56,000 bps using synchronous transmission. A second possibility is to use T-1 or fractional T-1 service if the lines exist already. If the T-1 lines do not exist or if the data transmission is too infrequent to warrant the purchase of T-1 multiplexers, there is still a third option.

It is possible to send information over a public data network which follows the international X.25 standard adopted by the Consultive Committee on International Telephone and Telegraph (CCITT). Sometimes referred to as a value-added network or packet switching network, it does offer a number of very valuable services.

As Figure 7-4 illustrates, a packet-switched network can utilize any of several different routes to connect two computers. Data is placed in packets containing special control information such as source and destination address. Since the network sends packets along whichever route happens to be available at any given moment, information segmented into several different packets likely will arrive out-of-order. A Packet Assembler/Dissambler handles the housekeeping necessary in proper sequencing of information.

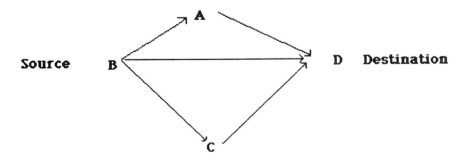

Figure 7-4 X.25 Traffic Can Take Different Routes

Figure 7-5 shows the types of service offered by public data networks. Information on packet networks can be converted from one protocol to another. In other words, an IBM mainframe computer can send a packet that is converted by the PDN to a format that Digital Equipment Corporation computer (DEC) can understand.

* **Electronic Mail**
* **Electronic Data Interchange (EDI)**
* **Encryption**
* **Asynchronous to Synchronous Protocol Translation**
* **Error Correction**
* **Facsimile Service**

Figure 7-5 Types of X.25 Services Offered

A major advantage of packet switched networks is that international links can transmit information to several international locations. Since the international X.25 standard is machine-independent, it can serve as a form of international mail for companies with world-wide operations and incompatible computers.

INTEGRATED
8 SERVICES DIGITAL
NETWORK (ISDN)

WHAT IS ISDN?

Integrated Services Digital Network (ISDN) represents the digitizing of our public telephone system so that it will be able to carry both voice and data at very high rates of speed. In Chapter 7 we looked at the T-carrier lines and saw that they provided high-speed data transmission; unfortunately, these lines are only economical for relatively short distances, assuming that the phone company already has the links installed. ISDN will permit the simultaneous transmission of voice, data, and video signals internationally as well as nationally. Already in beta test, ISDN will become a reality during the early 1990s. In this chapter we'll examine the basic components of ISDN.

The Advantages of ISDN

Before examining ISDN's components, let's take a few moments to look at some of its major advantages. For years ISDN has had the reputation of a major technological revolution that was "just around the corner" but never seemed to arrive. Industry experts could draw a laugh by calling it "It Still Does Nothing," "I Still Don't Know," or for the truly cynical, "I Smell Dollars Now."

Presumably, since ISDN will send integrated voice, data, and video signals over the same digital lines, users will get much faster, more efficient transmission of data than they do with analog modems, which usually provide a maximum transmission speed of 19.2 kbs.

Another advantage of ISDN is the true integration of the voice, data, and video streams of information. Users should be able to see a high-quality video picture on their monitors while a voice provides accompanying information.

Finally, ISDN should be more reliable from a strictly data-communications perspective because of better diagnostic and alternate routing capabilities, greater bandwidth flexbility, and easier routing of data internationally. Companies will know they can have cost-effective, reliable lines carrying data virtually anywhere. And that's why data communications managers are optimistic about ISDN.

Basic Rate Interface (BRI)

The Basic Rate Interface (BRI) is also called "2B + D." This interface, designed for the home and small business user, provides two "B" channels at 64 kbs and one packet-switched D channel at 16 kbs. The B channels will carry data, while the D channel is designed to carry control information.

The Primary Rate Interface (PRI)

Designed with large businesses in mind, the Primary Rate Interface (PRI) consists of 23 B channels, each of which operates at 64 kbs, and a D channel operating at 64 kbs. The European standard consists of 30 B + D or 30 64 kbs B channels and 1 64 kbs D channel so that the total channel provides a 2.048 transmission rate.

The HO Channel

ISDN also supports an HO channel consisting of six 64 kbs channels. The HO channel operates at a combined speed of 384 kbs and is designed for compressed video and high-speed fax transmission.

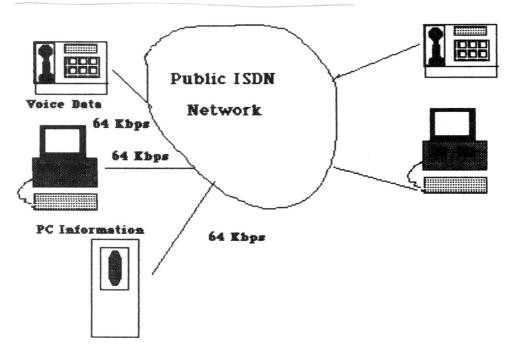

Figure 8-1 ISDN in Action

ISDN Gateways

The near future should see the introduction of ISDN gateways that serve as a way to send information from one network to another. Wide area networks that currently send information in asynchronous form at 19.2 kbs will be able to communicate at 64 kbs as illustrated in Figure 8-1.

THE BUILDING BLOCKS OF ISDN

Figure 8-2 illustrates the key components comprising the ISDN model; in this section we'll define them for you.

ISDN Terminals

ISDN terminals will be able to connect directly to a network channel termination unit (NT2) using what is called an "S" interface. Examples of NT2 units include PBXs, local area networks, and terminal controllers.

Non-ISDN Terminals

Non-ISDN terminals including all the present RS-232-C compatible equipment will need to be connected to special terminal adapters through what is called an "R" interface. The terminal adapters will support RJ11 plugs for voice and RS-232C, as well as V.35, and RS-449 interfaces for data.

Network Termination 1 Equipment

While Network Termination Equipment type 2 includes intelligent controllers and processors, Network Termination Equipment type 1 (NT1) consists of the functions associated with the physical and electrical termination of ISDN; in other words, the first-layer functions of the OSI model we discussed previously. NT1 and NT2 equipment are connected via the special T interface illustrated in Figure 8-2.

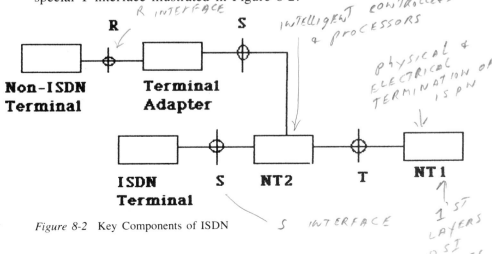

Figure 8-2 Key Components of ISDN

9 ■ NETWORK MANAGEMENT

WHAT IS NETWORK MANAGEMENT?

Simply put, network management means maintaining a network and ensuring its efficient operation. What makes this job so complicated is the sheer number of pieces that must fit together smoothly. We have seen in the first eight chapters that data communications transmission can involve mainframe computers and PCs, local area networks, modems and multiplexers, X.25 packet switching networks, and T-1 lines. Noise of any kind on any of these lines or cables can disrupt the data flow.

NETWORK MANAGEMENT FUNCTIONS

A network management system enables the network manager to monitor his or her network's operations, to report problems when they occur, and to generate detailed periodic reports. Network reconfiguration is another feature most managers want. Some network management systems also have the ability to take corrective action. This action might mean sending information along an alternative path until the reported problem can be corrected by the network manager. On a data network, one of the most useful tools for discovering why the network is not running at peak efficiency is the protocol analyzer.

Protocol Analyzers

The protocol analyzer can provide key information about the packets flowing around a network. It reports on the various types of errors found in a packet, the existence of "data runts" (packets caused by collisions), illegal network addresses, and a wide range of other conditions. Protocol analyzers also provide valuable network statistics on overall traffic patterns.

Network General's "The Sniffer" is an example of a protocol analyzer. It is a Compaq portable computer with protocol analyzer software and a special network adapter. As figure 9-1 illustrates, a protocol analyzer is a computer in its own right that attaches to a network and then monitors the flow of information. The protocol analyzer can be programmed using a number of "filters" so that just the right type of frames can be captured and interpreted. For example, it is possible to capture just those frames traveling between a file server and a specific workstation. When you analyze the information contained in these frames, it is possible to see not only which information reached the workstation, but also whether the workstation's network interface card was working properly.

Figure 9-1 A Protocol Analyzer Attaches Directly to a Network

MANAGEMENT OF AN INTEGRATED VOICE/DATA NETWORK

The trend today is toward integrated voice/data networks with the voice and data information flowing as bits along digital pathways. Very sophisticated network management systems are required to manage and control such operations. Since virtually every company large enough to have an integrated voice/data network is large enough to have been visited by an IBM and an AT&T account executive, let's examine very briefly what these two communications giants suggest as their network management solutions.

IBM's Solution: NetView

IBM's NetView is built around its mainframe computer environment and its System Network Architecture (SNA). All network management software runs on an IBM mainframe and virtually ties up that computer's processing capabilities. To facilitate communications with PBXs and non-IBM equipment, IBM developed NetView/PC, a program that runs on an IBM microcomputer and is capable of interfacing with PBXs and non-IBM computers and then sending its information to the mainframe computer running NetView. Figure 9-2 illustrates IBM's vision of how voice/data information can be gathered and then sent to the mainframe computer running NetView.

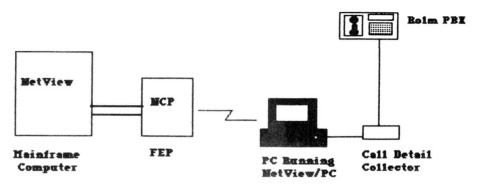

Figure 9-2 NetView in Action

AT&T's UNMA and the Accumaster Integrator

AT&T has taken a completely different direction in its network management product known as Unified Network Management Architecture (UNMA). UNMA is based on the OSI standards. AT&T developed an interface called Network Management Protocol (NMP) which it has provided to vendors so they may write programs that can use UNMA.

AT&T's approach is based on distributed processing, which means that network management is conducted on AT&T microcomputers and minicomputers in conjunction with AT&T modems and multiplexers. AT&T's Accumaster (pictured in Figure 9-3) is a PC-based administrative tool that permits network managers to monitor voice and data networks as well as T-1 lines.

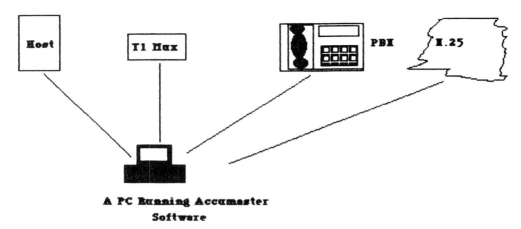

Figure 9-3 AT&T's UNMA & Accumaster

AND THE WINNER IS. . . .

As we move into the 1990s and integrated voice/data networks become more common, network management systems will become more popular. Many network managers are uncomfortable with IBM's lack of committment to the voice industry and AT&T's lack of success in the computer industry. They wonder if either giant can provide a complete network solution. Meanwhile other communications giants including DEC are developing their own network management products. It's much too early to pick a winner in an industry that is changing so rapidly. In fact, that's one reason data communications is such a fascinating topic. Isn't it?

ABOUT THE AUTHOR

Stan Schatt is just the person to write a book on basic data communications. His interests and professional experiences lend themselves perfectly to the topic. Dr. Schatt's background includes mainframe, minicomputer, and microcomputer experience. He helped develop assembly language programming training classes for Honeywell. Schatt also has had extensive minicomputer experience working for AT&T's Information Systems division. His microcomputer experience includes a stint as a General Manager of a leading microcomputer company. Dr. Schatt has served as the Chairman of the Telecommunications Department at DeVry Institute of Technology in Los Angeles where he helped develop curriculum in that exciting field and also taught a very popular introduction to computers course. Currently Schatt serves as the President of Network Associates, a Carlsbad based consulting and training firm. He also is an instructor for System Technology Forum's national seminars and Golden Gate's Telecommunications program. Schatt holds a PhD from the University of Southern California, Master's degrees from both Arizona State University and the American Graduate School of International Management, and a Bachelor's degree from Arizona State University.

Perhaps most of all, Schatt is a master teacher who brings that love of teaching to this book. The University of Southern California, University of Houston, and DeVry Institute of Technology have all cited him for outstanding teaching. Schatt even spent a year in Japan as a Fulbright Professor and taught at both Tokyo University and Keio University, Japan's equivalent of Harvard and Yale.

Schatt has written extensively in the field of data communications and telecommunications. Among his fifteen published books are *Microcomputers in Business and Society* (Merrill), *Voice/Data Telecommunications for Business* (Prentice-Hall), *Understanding Local Area Networks* (Howard W. Sams, Jr.), and *Understanding Novell's NetWare* (Howard W. Sams, Jr.).

When Schatt is not writing, teaching, or consulting, he likes to travel with his wife Jane who teaches first grade at Mission Estancia School. A few years ago they wrote a book together entitled *Bank Streeting Writing With Your Apple* which showed parents how to help their children become better writers using a word processing program. The Schatt household contains a Macintosh, an IBM compatible, and an old Kaypro computer. Their son, Dan, is a student at the University of California Santa Barbara campus where he uses his trusty Macintosh SE to write his term papers.

INDEX